Bible Stories

for

Children

By

John Marshall

For information about permission to reproduce selections from this book, write to Permissions. The Light and the Way Books.

6845 Elm Street, McLean Va. 22101

Visit our Web site: WWW. Litchfield Literary Books.Com

BIBLE STORIES For Children

SHORT SKETCHES OF THE BIBLE

SPECIALLY ILLUSTRATED FOR THE LITTLE PEOPLE

PREFACE

"The Children's Bible" provides, in simple English, a translation of selections from both the Old and the New Testament. These selections have been made as a result of more than twenty-five years of observation and study. The text is that of the Bible itself, but in the language of the child, so that it may easily be read to the younger children and by those who are older. It is not in words of one syllable, for while the child is reading the Bible he should gradually learn the meaning of new words and idioms.

The Bible contains the foundations on which the religious life of the child must be built. The immortal stories and songs of the Old and New Testaments are his richest inheritance from the past. To give him this heritage in language and form that he can understand and enjoy is the duty and privilege of his parents and teachers.

It is hoped that "The Children's Bible" will meet the need and the demand, which parents and educators alike have long felt and often expressed, for a simple translation of selections from the Bible most suited to the needs and the interests of the child. It is also believed that after the child has learned to appreciate and love these stories and songs, he will be eager and able to read the Bible as a whole with genuine interest and understanding.

CONTENTS:

FEEDING THE MULTITUDES.

Jesus had chosen twelve out of the many who flocked about Him wishing to be His disciples, and these twelve were called apostles. He sent them forth to preach the gospel, giving them power to cast out evil spirits and to heal diseases; and when they were about to go forth upon their mission, He gave them instructions regarding what they were to do, and warned them of the persecutions which would be heaped upon them. He also bade them be strong and not fear those who had power to kill the body only, because the soul was far more precious. So the apostles went out into the cities and towns and preached the word of God and carried blessing with them.

When they came back they told Jesus what they had done, and they went with Him across the sea of Galilee to a quiet spot where they could rest and talk over their work.

But the people went around the sea, or lake, to join them on the other side; and when Jesus saw the crowds He was sorry for them, and taught and healed them again as He had done so many times.

In the evening His disciples urged Him to send the people away that they might buy food for themselves in the village; but Jesus said, "Give ye them to eat."

The disciples thought this would be impossible. "We have here but five loaves and two fishes," they told Him; and when He said, "Bring them hither to Me," they obeyed Him with wonder.

Then Jesus commanded the people to sit down in groups upon the green grass; and He took the loaves and gave thanks to God for them, and broke them into pieces, handing them to His disciples to give to the people.

He divided the fishes also in the same way, and the disciples went about among the groups giving each person a share, and everyone had enough to eat; for although there were about five thousand men there, besides women and children, the food was sufficient for all. Even more than this, when the multitude had eaten all that they wanted, the disciples gathered up twelve baskets full of the broken pieces.

When the people saw this wonderful miracle which Jesus had done, they wished to make Him king at once, for they thought He was the Promised One for whom they had been so long waiting, and they did not know that the kingdom of Christ was not to be an earthly kingdom.

But Jesus would not allow them to make Him king, and He left them and went up on the top of a mountain alone.

On another occasion when a great crowd had gathered to hear Him and had been for a long time without food, He called His disciples to Him and told them that He felt very sorry for the people because they had been fasting three days, and He could not send them away so weak and hungry for fear they would faint before they could reach home.

But His disciples said they did not know where they could get food for so many, as they were in the wilderness.

Jesus asked them how many loaves of bread they had, and they told Him seven, and also a few small fishes.

Then Jesus bade the people sit down on the ground around Him, and He took the seven loaves and the fishes and offered thanks to God; afterwards, He broke the loaves into pieces as He had done before and gave them, with the fishes, to His disciples, and the disciples distributed them among the people. As they gave out the food it continued to increase wonderfully, so that all the people were fed; and even after that there was food enough left so that they took up seven baskets full, although about four thousand men, with many women and children, had eaten.

These miracles show not only the power of our Lord, but His tenderness and thoughtfulness for those around Him in the everyday affairs of life. He not only cared for the souls of His people, but for their physical comfort as well; for His heart was ever open to the cry of human need.

One of the first acts by which He manifested His power to the men who afterwards became His disciples, was an act of helpfulness.

He saw two ships by the Lake of Gennesaret with the fishermen near by washing their nets, and going aboard one of the ships, which belonged to Simon Peter, He asked him to put out a little way from land; then, when His request had been complied with, He taught the people from the ship.

After He had finished His teaching, He said to Simon, "Launch out into the deep and let down your nets for a draught." Simon told Him that they had worked all night and had caught no fish, but that they would do as He bade them.

And when they had done so, the net was filled so that it broke, and they had to call to their partners in the other ship to come and help them; and both ships were filled. Then Peter and James and John left all to follow Jesus.

JESUS CALMS THE TEMPEST.

At one time when Jesus had entered a ship to cross the Sea of Galilee with His disciples, a great storm arose and the waves nearly covered the little vessel, so that they were apparently in great danger.

The disciples were frightened, but Jesus was asleep and the storm did not disturb Him. As it grew worse and worse and the disciples became more than ever afraid, they went back to where Jesus lay and wakened Him, crying out, "Master, dost Thou not care that we perish?"

When they said this, Jesus arose and spoke to the winds and the sea, saying, "Peace, be still!" Then at once the wind went down and the sea became calm, and the hearts of the men were filled with wonder and still greater faith and awe, while they said to one another, "What manner of man is this, that even the wind and the sea obey Him?" They had not yet learned that Jesus had power over all things whenever He chose to exercise it.

At another time when the disciples had crossed the Sea of Galilee, expecting that Jesus would join them upon the other side, a storm came up, suddenly as before, and the waters were quickly piled up in great waves; for the lake was narrow and deep, and the storms usually burst in full fury with little warning, doing much harm before there was a chance to escape. At this time the disciples had hard work to row the boat against the wind, and it was tossed about here and there by the waves in the middle of the sea until, toward morning, Jesus went out toward it, walking upon the water.

When the disciples saw Him coming they thought it was a spirit and were frightened: but He spoke to them, saying, "Be of good cheer; it is I, be not afraid."

Then Peter said: "Lord, if it be Thou, bid me come unto Thee on the water."

Jesus said, "Come," and Peter stepped out upon the water and started toward the Master; but his faith was not strong enough, and as he began to sink he cried, "Lord, save me!"

Jesus stretched out His hand and held him up. "O thou of little faith," He said, "wherefore didst thou doubt?"

When Jesus came into the boat the storm ceased, and soon they reached the shore. Then the disciples worshiped Him and said, "Of a truth Thou art the Son of God."

RUTH AND NAOMI.

The story of Ruth and Naomi is one of the sweetest and most touching of all the Bible stories. It shows the beauty of unselfish devotion and constant love, and the happiness which they brought, and teaches a lesson which is very helpful to us all.

A long time ago, in the days of the judges of Israel, there was a famine in the land of Canaan, and a man named Elimelech, whose home was in Bethlehem, went with his wife Naomi and his two sons to live in Moab.

After they had been there a while Naomi's husband died, leaving her with the two sons. Then, by and by, the sons married, and their wives were very good to Naomi, and loved her. But it was only ten years before both of the sons died, and Naomi thought it was best for her to go back to her old home in Canaan; for she had been told that there was plenty in the land once more, and she wanted to see her own people and the relatives of her husband who was dead. So Naomi told her daughters-in-law to return to their own homes, because she could not expect them to be willing to leave everything for her sake.

"Go, each of you, to your mother's house," she said; "the Lord deal kindly with you as ye have dealt with the dead and with me." But they both wept and clung to her, saying, "Surely we will return with thee into thy land."

Naomi, however, thought they would be unhappy if they left their own country, and she urged them to stay there and let her go alone; so one of them kissed her over and over again and promised to do as she bade; but the other, who was named Ruth, would not leave her.

"Entreat me not to leave thee," she pleaded, "or to return from following after thee; for whither thou goest I will go, and where thou lodgest I will lodge; thy people shall be my people, and thy God my God; where thou diest I will die, and there will I be buried; the Lord do so to me and more, also, if aught but death part thee and me."

Then Naomi stopped urging her to return, and they went together to Bethlehem, where the friends of Naomi were very glad to welcome her and greeted her in a very friendly manner, saying again and again, "Is this Naomi?"

But she answered: "Call me not Naomi, but call me Mara, for the Almighty hath dealt very bitterly with me." She said this because Naomi means "pleasant" and Mara means "bitter," and the sorrowing widow felt that her life was a bitter rather than a pleasant one, since she had been bereaved of her husband and sons.

There lived in Bethlehem a man named Boaz, who was a relative of Naomi's husband, and who was also very wealthy. He had a large farm and many people, both men and women, worked in his fields, and as it was about the beginning of the barley harvest when the two women came to Bethlehem, these fields presented a busy appearance.

Ruth wished to do something to help support herself and her mother-in-law, so she begged Naomi to let her go into the fields and glean after the reapers—that is, to gather up the barley that was left after they had made up the sheaves—and Naomi told her that she might go.

Ruth happened to choose the field of Boaz to work in, and when the wealthy man came into the field and saw her, he said, "The Lord bless thee!" but he did not know who she was.

As he went away he inquired of the head reaper about the young woman, and afterward he said to Ruth: "Go not to glean in another field, but keep here close to my maidens." He also spoke to his young men about her, telling them to be kind and courteous to her, and he bade her go and drink of the water which they drew whenever she was thirsty.

When Ruth wondered at his kindness and asked him why he was so good to a stranger, he told her that he had heard of her love for Naomi and her unselfish devotion, and he said: "The Lord reward thee, and a full recompense be given thee of the Lord God of Israel, under whose wings thou art come to trust." He invited her also to sit with his reapers at meal-time, and he waited upon her that she might have enough to eat and drink.

When she had gone he commanded his young men to let her glean among the sheaves and to drop some handfuls purposely for her, and not to find fault with her or reprove her.

So Ruth worked in the field all day, and then beat out the barley which she had gleaned and took it to the city to show Naomi, who was very glad, indeed, and very thankful.

Naomi asked Ruth where she had gleaned, and when she had heard the whole story, she told her that Boaz was a near relative and that it was well for her to stay in his fields, as he had given her permission to do, until the end of the harvest. So Ruth kept close to the maidens who gleaned in the fields of Boaz until the end of both the barley and the wheat harvests.

Then one night when Boaz was to have a winnowing of barley, Naomi told Ruth to make herself ready, putting on her best clothing, and to go to the winnowing and the feast and to ask Boaz what she should do.

The winnowing is the fanning out of the straws from the kernels after the husks have been beaten off. A great many people helped about the work, and a feast was prepared for them.

Ruth did as Naomi had told her to do. When she had informed Boaz that she was a near relative he said, "Blessed be thou of the Lord, my daughter." Then he told her not to be afraid, but to bring the long veil which she wore, and when she had brought it he poured a large quantity of barley into it. She carried this to the city and gave it to her mother-in-law, telling her what Boaz had said, and Naomi was comforted; for she knew that Boaz would advise them wisely.

After this Boaz went to the city and consulted with the chief men and those that were interested in the welfare of Naomi and Ruth, and when he found that it would be wronging no one, he told the people that he was going to take Ruth for his wife, and the people said, "We are witnesses." So Boaz married Ruth; but in her new position as the wife of a very wealthy and influential man, this noble woman did not forget her love for Naomi, whom she still tenderly cared for. When a little son came to bless the union, Naomi rejoiced, for she felt almost as though it was her own little son, and she named him Obed and delighted in taking care of him.

When Obed became a man he married and had a son named Jesse, who in turn became the father of David, the great king of Israel. Jesus Himself was of the House of David, and so God's promise to His chosen people was fulfilled.

MOSES.

Pharaoh, the King of Egypt, had made a law that every boy baby of the Hebrew race should be killed, and there was great sorrow because of it. But when Moses was born, his mother managed to hide him for three months; then she made a cradle, or little ark, and putting him into it, carried him down to a river and hid the cradle among the reeds there.

Soon after this, Pharaoh's daughter came with her maidens to the river-side, and when she saw the beautiful child, she sent one of her maidens to bring it to her.

She took the little boy to the palace and named him Moses, and he became a great man among the Egyptians; he knew, however, that he belonged to the Hebrew race, and when he saw how badly his own people were treated, he tried to help them; but at last he was obliged to leave

Egypt, and became a shepherd, taking care of the flocks of a priest called Jethro. He also married Jethro's daughter.

After a time, God spoke to Moses out of a burning bush, and told him that he must go and rescue his people from the cruel Egyptians. Moses thought he could not do this; but God promised to help him, and to show him what he would be able to do with that help, God turned the rod which Moses carried into a serpent. Then God told Moses to pick the serpent up by the tail, and as he did so, it became a rod again. He showed him another sign, also; but Moses was still afraid, because he could not talk well and thought that Pharaoh would not listen to him. So God told him to take his brother Aaron for a spokesman.

Moses and Aaron, therefore, went into Egypt, where they called together the chief men among their own people, the Hebrews, or Israelites, and told them what God had commanded. Moses also did the miracles which God had given him power to do, and the people believed that God had sent him.

After this Moses and Aaron went to Pharaoh, and told him that it was the Lord's command that he should let the Israelites go. Pharaoh knew nothing about God, and became very angry, saying that Moses and Aaron kept the people from their work by telling them such things; and he treated the poor Israelites worse than before.

But Moses had faith in God; so he was able to perform before the king the wonderful things that he had done before his own people; still, Pharaoh would not let the children of Israel go.

Then Moses turned the waters of the rivers into blood; and after that he caused large numbers of frogs to run over the land and through the houses, doing great harm. He also brought locusts and other insects to be a pest to the people, and caused many of the useful animals which belonged to the Egyptians to grow sick and die, doing all these wonders with the rod which God had given him. But Pharaoh would not listen to him.

Then God commanded Moses again, and he brought other plagues upon the Egyptians; but Pharaoh would not give up.

At last, however, God sent a still more terrible trouble; for the first-born of every Egyptian family, and even the first-born among their flocks, died; although the Israelites, who were constantly praying to the Lord and making sacrifices, were spared, as they had been all the time.

Then Pharaoh was frightened into obeying God, and he let the Israelites go; so they started at once for the land of Canaan, and the Lord guided them by a cloud, which at night looked like a pillar of fire.

When the Israelites had reached the Red Sea, they found that Pharaoh was pursuing them with a large army. But God commanded Moses to stretch forth his rod over the sea; he did so, and the waters parted, making a high wall upon either side, so that the children of Israel passed through and reached the other side in safety. Pharaoh and his hosts followed and were all drowned.

When the children of Israel saw that they were safe, they sang a beautiful song of praise to God, and then they went on their way again.

After they had traveled for some time, they were in need of bread and meat, and they complained about Moses because he had brought them to a land where they had not enough to eat. But God sent them plenty of quails and also a substance which they could use for bread. Later, when they wanted water, the Lord commanded Moses, and he struck a rock with his rod, and pure water poured out of it, so that the thirsty people and their animals had all that they wanted.

In this way God took care of them as they journeyed through the new and strange country toward the promised land, and Moses became the law-giver of the Israelites, receiving his commandments from God.

JACOB AND ESAU.

Jacob and Esau were twin brothers, sons of Isaac and Rebekah. Esau was the dearer to his father; but Rebekah loved Jacob more, and she wished her favorite son to have the birthright, or larger portion of the property, which really belonged to Esau because he was a little the older.

One day Esau came in from hunting, very tired and hungry, and sold his birthright to Jacob for a kind of stew called pottage.

Afterward, when Isaac had grown very old, he sent Esau one day to get some of his favorite meat, saying that when he returned he should have his father's blessing.

But Rebekah heard this and determined that Jacob should have the blessing instead. So she prepared meat, then dressed Jacob in some of his brother's clothing, covering his hands and neck with the skin of the kids, and sent him to his father; and Isaac blessed him, for his sight was dim, and he thought it was Esau.

When the elder brother returned, he was very angry with Jacob, and Isaac was deeply grieved to think he had been deceived; but he blessed Esau as well, who became prosperous and had large possessions and great power.

After this Jacob went to his mother's people, where he met Rachel, whom he loved very dearly. He told Laban, her father, that he would serve him faithfully seven years if Rachel might be his wife, and Laban consented to this; at the end of the seven years, however, he told Jacob that he must first marry Leah, as she was the older, but if he would serve another seven years he might have Rachel also. So Jacob served another seven years for Rachel, and then they were married.

Later Esau and Jacob met and were very glad to see each other, for Jacob had repented of his sin, and God had forgiven him; while Esau forgave him also.

THE APOSTLE PAUL.

Before his conversion to the faith of Christ, Paul was called Saul, and he persecuted the Christians, believing that they were doing wickedly and that he ought to punish them for it.

But while he was in the midst of these persecutions, and as he was journeying toward Damascus one day, he saw suddenly at noon-time, a light shining in the heavens which was greater than the light of the sun, and he and all that were with him fell to the earth in wonder and awe. Then Saul heard a voice speaking to him and saying, "Saul, Saul, why persecutest thou Me?" And Saul said, "Who art Thou, Lord?" And the voice answered, "I am Jesus, whom thou persecutest."

Then Saul was instructed as to what he was to do, and was told that he would become a minister of Christ. From that time Paul preached and taught the Christian religion, and converted many people to it.

But he was persecuted in his new work as he had persecuted others, being finally taken prisoner and threatened with scourging; he declared himself a Roman citizen, however, and therefore safe from such treatment, and went on openly confessing his faith and telling of his conversion, and he appealed for protection to the Roman emperor.

He was then put on board a ship as a prisoner to be taken to Rome. While they were at sea a violent storm came up, and Paul warned the sailors that they were in great danger; but they would not listen to him. At last the ship was wrecked, all on board being cast ashore upon an island, whither they had been carried, clinging to boards and broken pieces of the ship.

The barbarous people of the island treated them kindly, building a fire that they might dry their clothing and get warm; for it was cold and they were, of course, drenched.

The men were very glad to be safe once more; but a strange thing happened after a little: Paul gathered up an armful of sticks to put upon the fire, and as he placed them upon the flames, a viper, which is a kind of poisonous snake, came out of the bundle and clung to his hand; he shook it off into the fire, however, without the slightest sign of fear.

Those who were about him thought that the hand would swell and that Paul would die from the effects of the bite, and they watched him closely, believing that this trouble was sent to him as a punishment for his sins. But no evil results came from the wound, and then the barbarians thought he was a god and looked upon him with great respect.

Paul and the men who were with him remained upon the island for three months. At the end of that time they went away in a ship, finally reaching Rome, where the prisoners were given up to the authorities; but Paul was allowed to live by himself, with only a soldier to guard him, and after a while he called the chief men of the Jews together and told them why he was there and preached to them the Word of God. His preaching was received by some with faith, but others did not

Paul went on preaching and teaching in Rome for two years, living in a house which he hired, and he brought many to Jesus. He was a man of excellent education and a powerful preacher. His Epistles, given in the Bible, are full of power and the fire of conviction, and he did a wonderful work for the great cause in which he believed with all his heart.

Paul was physically small and deformed; but mentally he was a giant. He had been taught the knowledge of the Romans, and was therefore well fitted to take up this new cause in a manner which would appeal to educated people as well as to those who had no learning.

From the time of his conversion until his death he labored faithfully in the ministry of Christ, fearing no persecution or hardship when he could do the Master's bidding and teach His holy will. The work which he did was a wonderful work, and his influence in the Christian world has been a very remarkable one. Brave, untiring, devoted to the cause of Christ, he at last lost his life in that cause, adding another to the list of martyrs whose memory the world loves and reveres.

The story of Paul's experiences reads like those tales of adventure which are so full of absorbing interest that when once they have been taken up, we do not feel like laying them down again until they are finished.

This is true also of many others of the Bible stories, and great authors have taken their themes from them for the writing of books which have become famous.

The more we study the Bible, the more wonderful it becomes, and the more we learn that in that marvelous book are set forth nearly all the experiences of which human life is capable, with the teaching which each of these experiences should bring and the lesson to be learned by the reading of them. In all the world there is not another collection so wonderful as this.

DAVID.

David, the son of Jesse, was a beautiful boy, who could charm by his wonderful music. But he was to be more than a "sweet singer," for Samuel, the prophet of the Lord, declared that he should be King of Israel, and poured the sacred oil upon his head.

Saul, who was then the King of Israel, had spells of insanity, and David was sent for to try and calm him by his music. In this he was so successful that after a time the king seemed to be entirely cured; so David returned to his home, and staid there quietly until his father sent him to the camp of the Israelites, with food for his brothers.

He found Saul's army in great commotion, because Goliath, a mighty warrior of the Philistines, had come out before both armies and had offered to fight any man who should be sent against him.

Goliath had a cap of brass on his head, and his body was well protected with a covering of iron and brass, while he carried a monstrous spear and sword, and a heavy shield. As he came before the two camps, he cried out: "I defy the armies of Israel this day; give me a man, that we may fight together!"

When David came up and heard the story, he said: "Who is this Philistine, that he should defy the armies of the living God?" And David offered to go forth against Goliath.

So he went out in his shepherd's dress, with only his staff and sling; and Goliath, who was very angry at this, cried out: "Am I a dog, that thou comest against me with a staff?" Then he began to make fun of David. But David answered: "Thou comest against me with a sword and a shield; but I come against thee trusting in the Lord of Hosts, the God of Israel, whom thou hast defied."

Then, as Goliath came nearer, David took a stone from the bag at his side, and putting it into his sling, he took good aim, and it struck Goliath in the middle of the forehead and stunned him. As the giant fell, David ran up to him, and taking the mighty sword, cut off his head with it.

This act of David's brought a great victory to Saul's army, and the king was delighted with his courage; while Jonathan, Saul's eldest son, loved the boy from that time, and they became like brothers. David also married the daughter of Saul, and was placed over his men of war.

But when all the people praised David, and Saul knew how much they loved him, he grew jealous, and David was obliged to fly for his life and hide himself from the king. During these wanderings, he wrote some of his most beautiful psalms.

Saul, however, was finally killed, and at last David became king. He ruled Israel for nearly forty years, making it a great and powerful nation; and when he died he was buried at Jerusalem, which was called "The City of David," because he had caused it to be taken from the enemy.

THE TOWER OF BABEL.

The sons of Noah were named Shem, Ham and Japheth. These sons in turn became the fathers of children so that the descendants of Noah were very numerous.

One of these descendants, named Nimrod, was a mighty hunter and a man of power and authority in the land, and it has even been said that the people worshiped him as a god.

In those days men liked to build high towers reaching away up toward the heavens. Perhaps they were afraid of another flood, and perhaps they simply wished to show what they could do; but however that may be, ruins of towers can still be seen in various parts of the world, one of the most noted of which is that of the "Tower of Nimrod." It is forty feet high and stands on the top of a hill near the River Euphrates in Asia.

In the time of Nimrod, the people said, "Let us build us a city and a tower, whose top may reach unto Heaven; and let us make us a name, lest we be scattered abroad upon the face of the whole earth." So they began to build the tower, and they made it very strong indeed, and kept raising it higher and higher toward the heavens, thinking, Jewish tradition, or story, tells us, that they would have a shelter in which they would be perfectly safe from any flood which might come, or any fire. There were some of the people also who wished to use the tower as a temple for the idols which they worshiped. Six hundred thousand men worked upon this wonderful tower, so the story goes on to say, and they kept up the work until the tower rose to a height of seventy miles, so that, toward the last, it took a year to get materials for the work up to the top where the laborers were employed. Of course this story is exaggerated, but without doubt the tower rose to a great height and was a wonderful piece of work.

God was not pleased with what the people were doing, however, because they thought themselves so great and powerful that they had no need of Him, and so He put an end to their bold plans.

Up to this time all the people of the world had spoken the same language; but now, when they were working upon this wonderful tower, they commenced to talk in different tongues so that they could not understand each other, and there was great confusion. Owing to this, they were obliged to give up the building of the tower, and they separated themselves into groups, or divisions, each division speaking the same language, and then they spread out over the world, forming the various nations.

The tower was called the Tower of Babel because of the babel, or confusion, of tongues which had taken place there, and it was left unfinished to be a monument of God's power and man's weakness without Him.

These men were skillful in building, else they never could have gone as far as they did in their stupendous work, and God was willing that they should exercise their skill, as He is willing that people shall do now; but when they thought themselves equal to Him, they learned how weak they really were in comparison. The story teaches the great lesson of dependence upon God and submission to His will and His laws.

THE BOYHOOD OF JESUS.

There are many beautiful stories of child-life, but the story of the Boyhood of Jesus is the most beautiful of all. It teaches a wonderful lesson of obedience to parents and love and respect for them, as well as of the charm of a pure and consecrated childhood, and

the lesson is all the more helpful because it is full of the human interest of everyday life.

Although the boy Jesus was gifted with a wisdom far beyond His years—a wisdom which was His because He was the Son of God, yet He lived much as other boys lived, doing the tasks that were given Him by His parents and being subject to them in all things.

Probably the people around Him did not think very much about what He said or did during those years. When they saw Him helping Joseph, the carpenter, or doing the little things which Mary, His mother, bade Him do, He seemed much like other little boys to them; they thought Him bright and pleasing, and it may be that there was something in His looks and in His manner which puzzled them, which set them to thinking of holy things in a wondering way; but Mary was the only one who dwelt upon the mystery of His life with a constant prayerful questioning as to just what the meaning of it was.

Mary treasured all His sayings in her heart and believed that the time would come when everyone would know that He was not simply an ordinary child like those around Him.

After Joseph had brought his family back from Egypt because, now that Herod was dead, it was safe for them to come into their own country again, they lived in the city of Nazareth, and so the words of the old prophets were true, that Jesus, the Savior of the World, should be a Nazarene, or dweller in Nazareth.

Every year the Jews held a feast at Jerusalem called the Feast of the Passover, in memory of the time when God passed over, or spared, His chosen people in Egypt, although He destroyed the first-born of the Egyptians. When Jesus was twelve years old He went to Jerusalem with Joseph and Mary to attend this feast.

There were many of the relatives and friends of the family there, and when they started home after the feast, there was probably some confusion about getting the company under way, for they traveled in a train consisting of people on foot and mounted upon donkeys, and they had, of course, some needful provisions to take with them, together with the things which they had brought for their comfort upon the journey and during their stay in Jerusalem; and as the parents of Jesus did not think of

His remaining behind, they neglected to look for Him, supposing He was somewhere in the train; so, when they had traveled for a day on the return trip, they were greatly surprised and troubled to find that He was missing.

They immediately started back for Jerusalem, wondering as they went what could have happened to their boy and fearful about it; but after three anxious days they found Him in the temple talking with the learned men there, listening to their wise words, and asking questions which astonished everybody who heard them, because they were full of an understanding of holy things that was not to be expected of a boy. When His parents had found Him, Mary said to Him, sorrowfully, "Son, why hast Thou dealt thus with us? Thy father and I have sought Thee sorrowing."

Then Jesus turned to her with sad and gentle respect, and asked, "How is it that ye sought Me? Wist ye not"—that is, "Do you not know"—"that I must be about My Father's business?"

Perhaps in these words He tried to give them an insight into the great meaning of His life; but they were puzzled, although Mary dimly felt all that He would have her understand. He did not at this time, however, explain to them further regarding what was in His own heart. It may be that He did not yet fully comprehend just what He was to do. He had taken upon Himself the human nature which He was to raise to something grander and nobler than human nature had ever been before, and in becoming a little child like other little children, perhaps it was God's plan that He should not yet have the judgment of a man in all things.

However that may have been, He went back with His parents and obeyed them as before, for the time had not come for Him to leave them and begin His teaching, except as He taught by the force of a beautiful example. But that example formed a great part of the purpose for which He was sent into the world, because one of the noblest truths that He impressed upon humanity was the duty of children to parents. His own life taught this better than any sermon could have done, for in all the history of the world we have no better example of what a child's conduct should be toward his parents. It is the more beautiful because Jesus was not like other children, but, having the wisdom of God in His heart, was far better able to judge for Himself between right and wrong.

During all these years Jesus grew in stature as well as in wisdom, and those around Him felt, without understanding it, that in some way He was different from the rest. The divinity of His nature could not be hidden, even in those early years, but it shone through all the small acts of everyday life, making them beautiful; while every one who knew Him was better and happier for coming near such a noble nature.